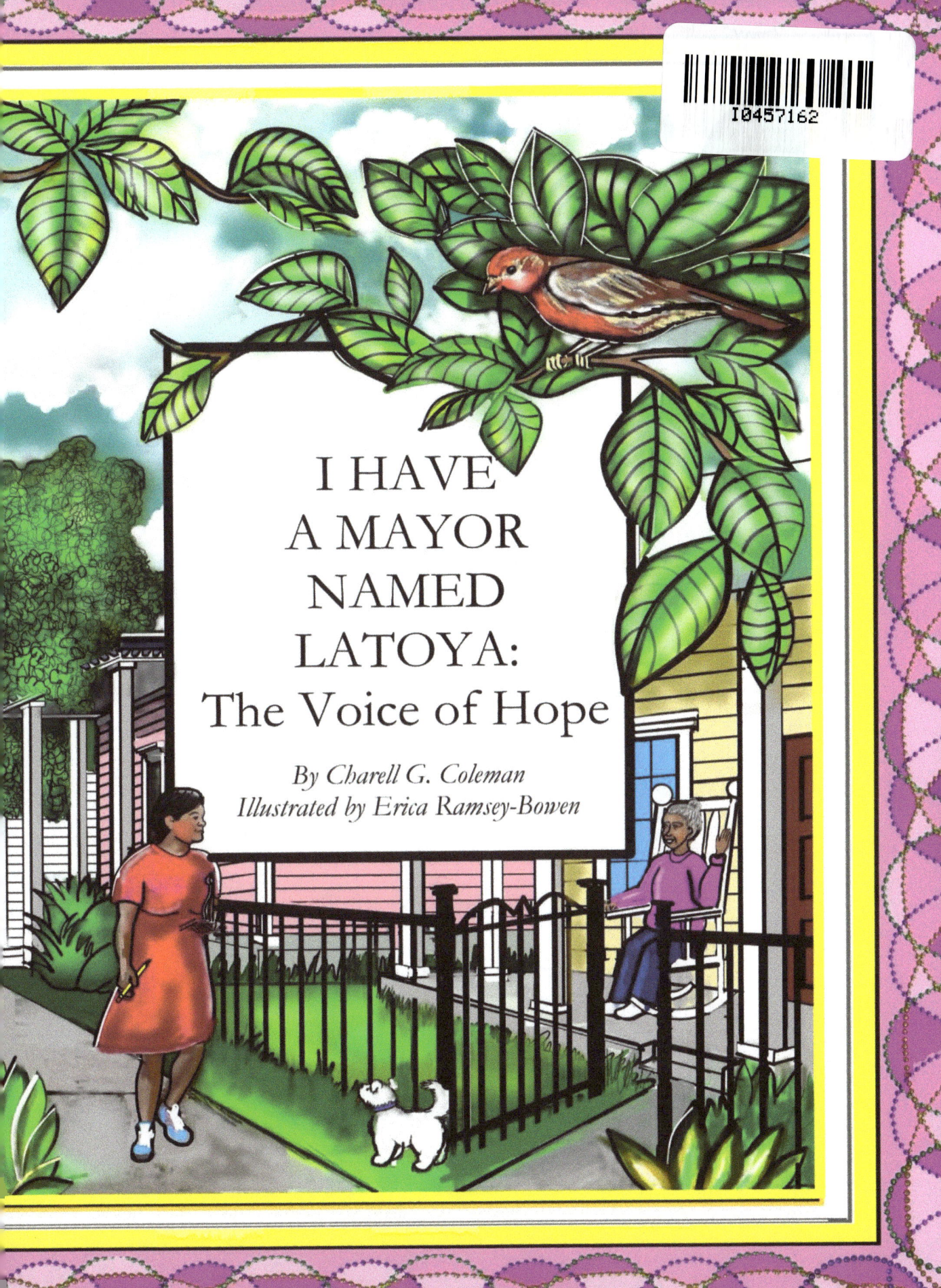

I HAVE A MAYOR NAMED LATOYA:
The Voice of Hope

By Charell G. Coleman

Illustrated by Erica Ramsey-Bowen

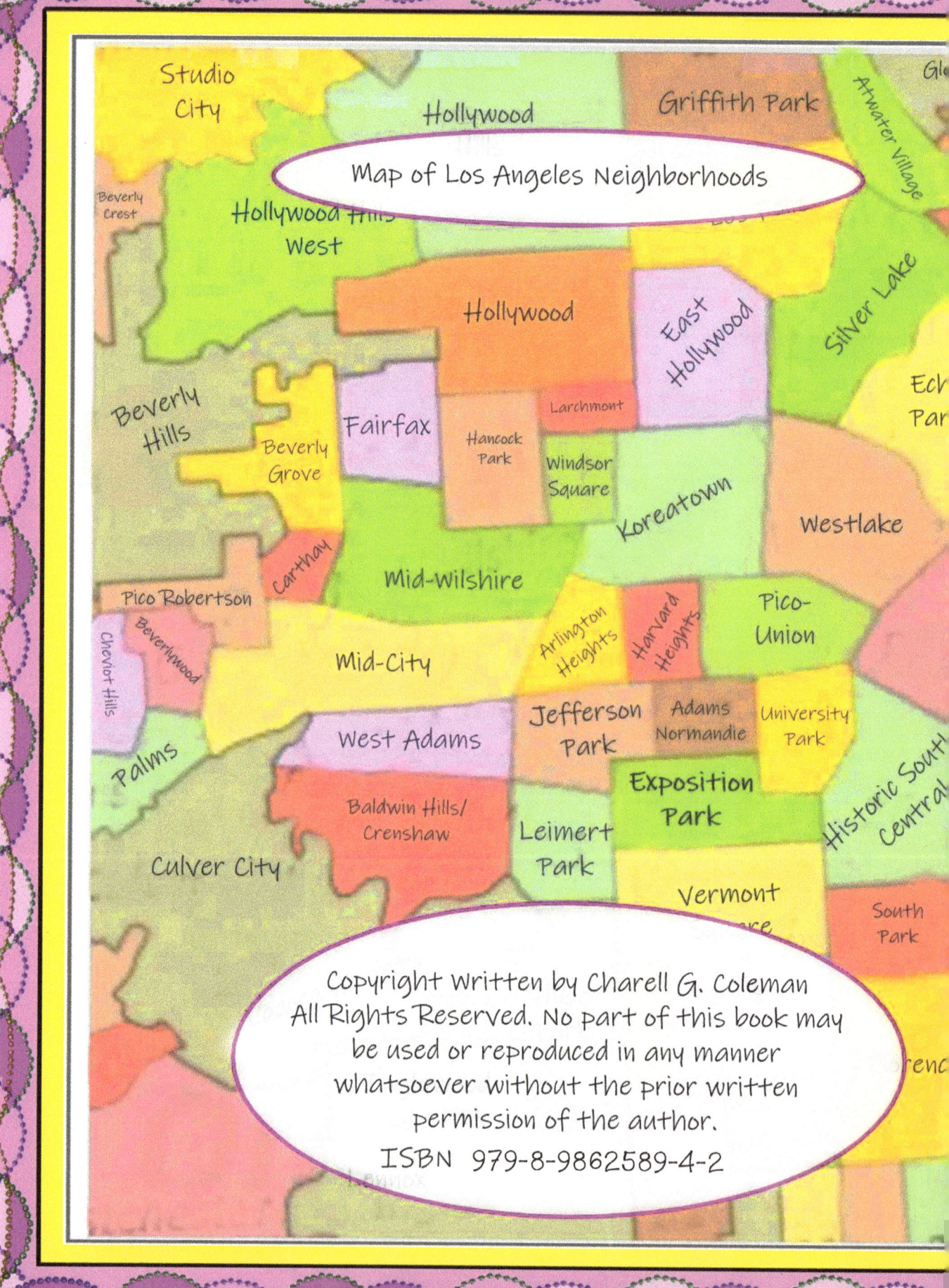

Map of Los Angeles Neighborhoods

ISBN 979-8-9862589-4-2

DEDICATION:

This book is dedicated to the citizens of New Orleans who suffered through the destruction of Hurricane Katrina, civil unrest and the pandemic.

Although many People of Color (black and brown) suffered at disparate rates, and lost many loved ones, Civil Service continued as an effort to rebuild the city.

Our greatest learning being we are stronger together as ONE!

#NOLA Strong

#City of Yes

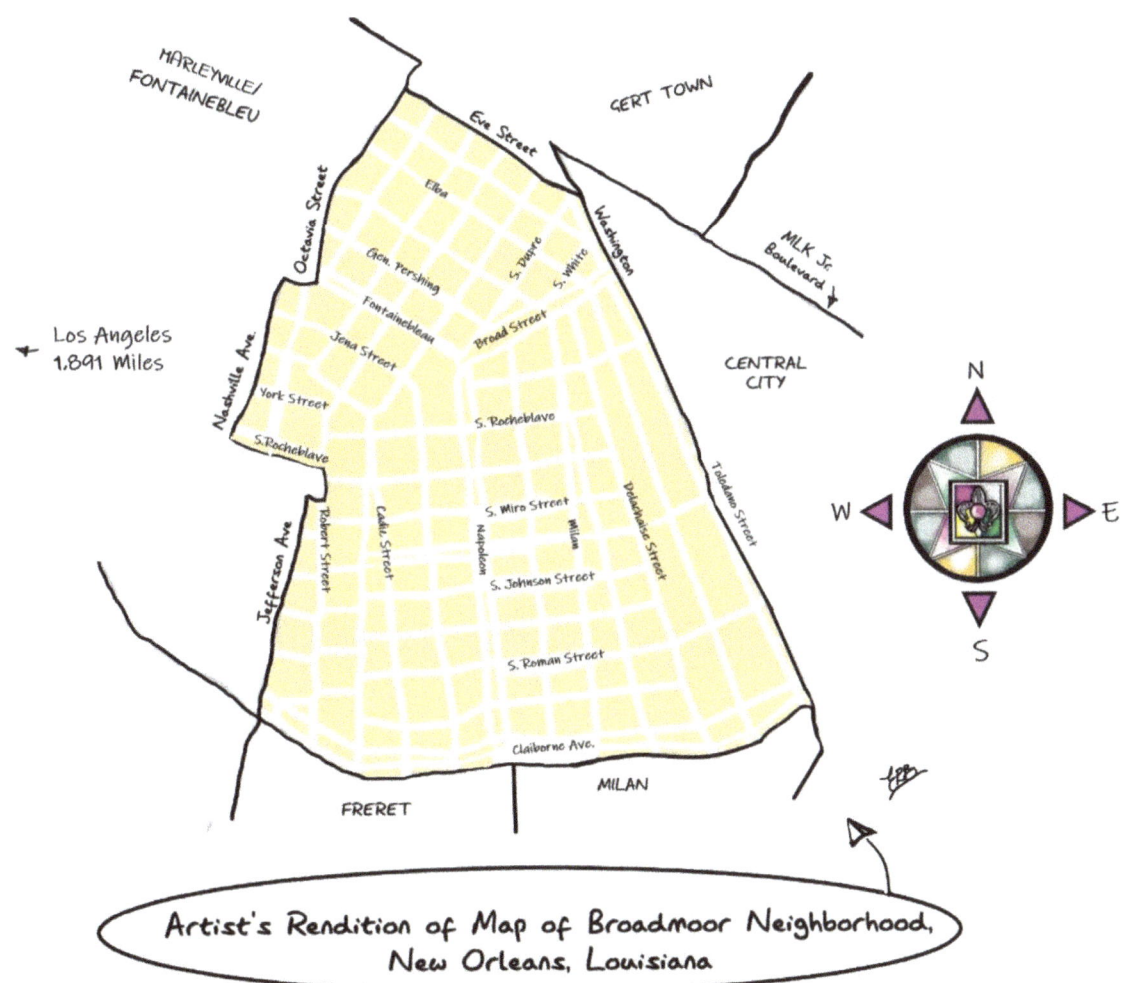

Artist's Rendition of Map of Broadmoor Neighborhood, New Orleans, Louisiana

Hope started long before I was born.

My grandmother's sister was one of the first black women to own a business in Los Angeles, California.

When I was a little girl, it seemed everyone was so happy.

I learned a lot from attending neighborhood meetings with my grandmother.

I had no idea how this would serve me later in life.

Mostly I learned that people in political offices had the power to affect change!

When I was four years old,
Jimmy Carter became the 39th
President of the United States of
America.

As a young child, I remember all the
fun we had because there were
social programs available for those
who may not have had a lot of
resources.

By the time I was 8 years old,
a new president was elected.
The fun seemed to go away.

Drugs and gangs began to take over
neighborhoods.

The rate of violence increased.

Things were changing.

My mom was a social worker until she was laid off of her job. My stepfather was a police officer until he began using drugs.

This caused him to make poor choices.

Because my Mom and Dad had to divorce, we no longer lived together. Our lives changed.

I also didn't feel well often.
I constantly had asthma attacks because Los Angeles was smoggy.

I always felt the need to help others and educate them just as my grandmother did for me.

When times got really tough, I was sent to live with her in Palmdale, California.

This was an effort to help my mother cope with the stress of being a single mother with few resources to live.

I always felt confident, until I joined so many brown people that looked just like me at Xavier University.

Somehow now I felt insecure.

I began to call upon my faith and tell myself that I was just as good as anyone else.

Today I share these same words with youth across the city of New Orleans.

Grandma and I went to the neighborhood meetings often.

That is where I trained to be a community organizer.

At the age of 13, I became Secretary of our local Chamber of Commerce.

I suppose politics started rather early for me.

Family has always been important to me. We traveled to see some of our family in Alabama during the summers.

Knowing my maternal grandmother ran a small business gave me confidence to lead.

Patrons at Grandmother's Store

GROCERY

Once as we passed through
New Orleans on a visit,
I saw the most beautiful city
and knew one day I would call
it home.

Leading the efforts to save Broadmoor as President of the Broadmoor Improvement Association after the devastation of Hurricane Katrina in 2005 showed us what true resilience was.

We were able to convince residents. to rebuild Broadmoor rather than allow a park to take its place.

Raising $5 million in pledges to rebuild was no small feat! Hooray for the Teamwork!

Trying to help rebuild Broadmoor was a major task but I knew anything was possible if I had the support of the people.

People from all walks of life were eager to help.

Election day expressed it BEST!

Small steps count. To think that my great aunt was appointed by President Lyndon B. Johnson to be an Ambassador of Consumer Affairs under his administration was a huge honor.

It was there the bridges were being built.

Being a mother has been one of the most important things on my agenda since RayAnn was born.

When she asked what would happen if I became Mayor, as her mother, I told her that would only mean she would have a desk in my office so that I could oversee her completing her school assignments in the evenings.

I value future generations and as a mother I care about their future.

The people know that I am 'Auntie Teedy.'

Love Makes The World Go Round

Mayoral Daughter Desk

As an African American, I acknowledge the struggles of our people. Finding ways to support entrepreneurs, artists and hard working citizens is important to me.

Education certainly plays an important role. Supporting Historically Black Colleges and Universities is part of securing the future for our youth as well.

Just as I want opportunities for our youth to thrive in the future, I believe in preserving the unique past and rich culture of New Orleans.

New Orleans architecture and historical sites and buildings have such a layered history. Helping to preserve this history is part of my job!

Sometimes being at the top means being lonely, but I know I have supporters just around the corner! Seeing friendly faces and keeping a journal helps!

I am honored to be New Orleans' Mayor and hope every young lady knows that they should never let others define them!

All young ladies are capable of reaching their aspirations as long as they are willing to do the work it takes to get there!

The future starts with every resilient girl and in my own household, it starts with my own, RayAnn.

HELP NOW STRATEGIES!!

WAYS TO HELP YOU GET BACK TO YOUR RESILIENT ZONE

Find 6 colors in the room. Think of something each one reminds you of that is pleasant

Take time to NOTICE the sounds in your room, outside or in a song

19

HELP NOW STRATEGIES!!

WAYS TO HELP YOU GET BACK TO YOUR RESILIENT ZONE

Count backwards from 25 while you walk the room

Drink a cup of water, juice or tea. Notice the process of swallowing each time.

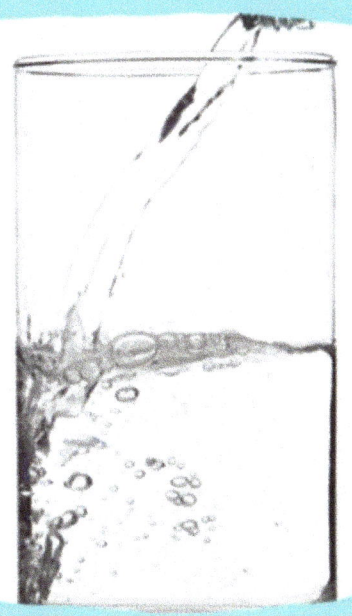

HELP NOW STRATEGIES!!

The Help Now! Skills involve specific strategies to bring down activation within the nervous system when a person is stuck in either the high or low zone. These strategies help the person focus on something else besides the distress and the sense of being overwhelmed. These strategies are used to activate other parts of the body and brain that help the person come back into balance.

TRAUMA RESOURCE INSTITUTE

Community Resiliency Model
Certified Teacher
Charell G. Coleman

ABOUT THE AUTHOR

Charell G. Coleman is a dedicated educator of 23 years, a Trauma Resiliency Institute Community Resiliency Model (CRM)® Certified Teacher, a mentor, a public speaker, and author of The Brown Girl Resilience Book Collection.
She has effectively transmuted her personal childhood trauma into a passion for teaching others wellness skills - the same skills that catapulted her into her own resilience zone and a successful, happy life! Her collection of books pays homage to the struggles of People of Color (black and brown), while sharing their inspiring stories of trials and resilience.

She writes and speaks to audiences about her core passions: Erasing Illiteracy, Educating Others About Executive Functioning Skills, and Healing Trauma From the Inside Out. Because of her expertise and warmth with all audiences, Charell has been featured on many Educational forums!

In addition to spending time with her husband and children, Charell's favorite past times include serving others through activities and programs through her local chapter of the illustrious sorority, Delta Sigma Theta, Incorporated.
She is also a Runner Girl who challenges herself to several 5K runs throughout the year -if she isn't busy reading a good book!

Learn more about Charell and what is next for her at: **www.LeadandInk.com.**

ABOUT THE ILLUSTRATOR

Erica Ramsey-Bowen resides in Atlanta, Georgia, but claims Pointe Coupee Parish, Louisiana, as her "Maison Deux". Her illustrative work is described as "whimsical and playful", and always created with the intention of bringing joy, information, and hope to the World.

She continues to partner with incredible non profits on key projects to help raise awareness of issues close to her heart; child safety, elder abuse prevention, environmental preservation, and the critical need for diversity, inclusion, and representation in children's literature.

Past and current amazing organizations Erica has worked with/for include Atchafalaya Basinkeeper, Chattanooga Aquarium Project & Personal Development, Zoo Atlanta, the Humane Society of Cobb County, and now, to her delight, the Brown Girl Resilience Collection of books by Author Charell G. Coleman.

She is a vibrant member of the Rotary Club of East Cobb, Georgia, the Louisiana Tri-Parish Alumnae Chapter of Delta SigmaTheta, Incorporated, a Board Member of CAP PD, and when she isn't dreaming up new stories or creating illustrations, enjoys hiking with her dog and husband.

You can see more of Ericas work at: litlebayoufairy.com or on Instagram: @Cre8WhatYouWish.